Laura's Rose:

The Story of Rose Wilder Lane

Rose Wilder Lane

Centennial Edition
1886-1986

by William T. Anderson

FOREWORD

This booklet **Laura's Rose: The Story of Rose Wilder Lane** is an answer to the countless persons who have asked, or written questions about Laura Ingalls Wilder's only child. Almost daily, summer by summer, as I serve as tour guide and host at the restored Ingalls homes in DeSmet, South Dakota, I'm asked about Rose. Similar is the situation in Mansfield, Missouri, Wilder Museum director Irene V. Lichty tells me. As our visitors file past the exhibits of Rose's furniture and belongings in DeSmet and Mansfield, they invaribly want to know about the fascinating life and career of the daughter whose mother they already know so well— Laura of the "Little House" books.

The material in this booklet and indeed, some of the writing, is actually condensed from two research papers I did while an undergraduate at Albion College in Michigan. The latter of these, several hundred typed pages, was super-vised and carefully "scrutinized" to my great advantage by Dr. Elizabeth R. Hosmer at Albion. I offer her my great thanks.

The facts of Rose's adventuresome, successful, brimful life I owe to many. Irene V. Lichty and her late husband, L. D., have always been generous in information exchange. Roger Lea MacBride, who called Rose "Grandma," has sup-plied me with many details in our conversations and in a voluminous exchange of correspondence. Rose herself, though reticent to discuss herself in relation to her mother's books, often supplied me with insight into her own character and personality in our correspondence. Thanks are also due to the late Berta and Elmer Hader, Rose's good friends; to Norma Lee Browning who says that "Rose taught me to write;" to Rose's Texas neighbor, Mrs. E. D. Giffen and to P. K. Slocum, rare book dealer, who has done wonders in obtaining many of Rose's out-of-print books and magazine articles for me.

W. T. A.
May, 1976

LAURA'S ROSE: The Story of Rose Wilder Lane

I. PRAIRIE CHILD

"I am personally a pioneer," Rose Wilder Lane wrote many years after her birth on a cold winter day in her parents' lonely little claim shanty on the snow-buried prairie near DeSmet, South Dakota.* Her assertion was no idle boast. From her earliest babyhood Rose's surroundings were those of the Dakota pioneer. The struggling saplings of her father's tree claim, the acres of yellowing grain and grass, the immense bowl of a sky and the intense sun were indelibly etched upon the child's awareness.

Even if Rose had grown up in the midst of a big city, her claim to pioneer traces would be valid by osmosis alone. Her father, Almanzo James Wilder, came from a long line of people journeying west; the first Wilders had come from England not long after the Mayflower sailed and ever since they had been journeying west. Almanzo, better known as "Manly" was born in upper New York state, but as a young man he had come west with his family to Spring Valley, Minnesota. From there young Manly had ventured into the endless prairie land of eastern Dakota Territory. There, in the little town of DeSmet, he had met, courted and married Rose's mother, Laura Elizabeth Ingalls.

Laura's family were pioneers too. From Wisconsin they had journeyed when Laura was almost too small to remember, into the wilds of Indian Territory. They moved north again to the banks of Plum Creek on the wheatlands of western Minnesota and then to Iowa. Finally, when Laura was almost grown, her father finally settled where Almanzo Wilder had—"where the west began"— in South Dakota.

"I chose the most wonderful of parents," Rose said

---

*Rose Wilder Lane, the first child of Laura and Almanzo Wilder, was born on a blustery Monday night, December 5, 1886. She shares her birthdate and year with the grandfather of the author of this book.

when she was grown and on her own. "My mother loves courage and beauty and books; my father loves nature, birds, and trees and curious stones, and both of them love the land, the stubborn, grudging, beautiful earth that wears out humans lives year by year. They gave me something of all these loves, and whenever I do something I really can't help sitting down and admiring, I always come plump up against the fact that I never would have done it if I hadn't been wise enough to pick out these particular parents."

Rose's description of her mother and father came years after her first days on the prairie were merely memories, but thanks to her mother's sister, Rose's Aunt Grace, we have a few snatches of description of the baby girl. Grace, at ten, was a faithful diarist and when her niece was just a month old she had this to say: "I think everything of Laura's baby. She is . . . just beginning to smile." A few months later, Grace wrote of Rose . . . "Rose is a big, fat baby but just as pretty. Laura was over a week ago and put Rose into short dresses."

There is little doubt that Rose was a much-loved and admired baby among her family. Most of her father's family were far away in Minnesota, but her mother's relatives, the Ingalls family, were comfortably nearby to watch and enjoy Rose's growth and progress. There were three aunts, Mary, Carrie and Grace, and Laura's parents, her Pa and Ma, took considerable pride in their first grandchild. As for Laura and Almanzo, Rose — named for the prairie roses which blanketed the prairies in June—this little daughter was a treasure beyond value. As Laura observed, a Rose in December was much rarer than a rose in June! Imagine her horror when poor childless Mr. and Mrs. Boast proposed the trade of little Rose for his best horse. Laura pitied these good friends, but all she could do was to urge Manly to drive off as soon as he could!

For Rose, experiences as a prairie child began as soon as her parents took her out of the warm little homestead house on the hill a mile north of DeSmet. One winter day, well wrapped, Rose was taken to visit her Grandma and Grandpa Ingalls; that day she knew how it felt to ride in a cutter when the thermometer read fifteen below. When spring came, Rose went right along with her parents to the fields and garden. In a clothesbasket she slept contentedly or looked at the shimmering blue sky above her. She learned to feel and see the lush prairie grass and she heard the meadowlark's song. When haying time came, Rose watched the activity from a safe spot beneath a windrow of hay. Learning to know her environment was not a matter of discovery from Rose; she merely grew up with the prairie all around her in its various moods and appearances.

The happy lives of Laura, Almanzo and Rose were marred rather harshly when Rose was just a year and a half old. Her parents had diphtheria. Rose was quickly swept away to the safety of the Ingalls home in De Smet, while her parents fought the battle with the disease. She escaped the illness herself, but was terrified, for her parents were expected to die. She asked questions and her usually gentle Grandma answered them with a "Hush!"— until Rose asked no more. Laura and Almanzo finally recovered, but Rose was still kept in town at the Ingalls' home. There were still problems: Almanzo was "stricken" with a relapse and a stroke, which paralyzed him. It seemed as though he would never again walk. "Grandma almost scolded about that, to the aunts. Bound and determined to get out and take care of the stock, he was. Now he would be bedridden all his days and what would Laura do? With Rose on her hands, besides." That talk filled Rose's mind. She could not find the words just yet for the hard realities — "gramma," "grampa," "bread and butter," and "cracker" were the limit of her vocabulary, but she comprehended much more than anyone could understand.

Rose's father, through will-power and Laura's help, began to recover slowly. It was fight to do the chores, to fasten the reins and plow the fields that spring, but Almanzo did what had to be done. After several dry years, he was determined to make a crop that would make life easier to bear. But the crop failed.

Although the prairie sun burned everything to yellow

and brown and orange and the hot winds blew and rushed over the land, Rose grew lustily. Already Laura could sense something special about her girl, a wonderful spark and flash and a thirst for knowledge and experiences. The sterility of the flat, dry land did nothing to stop Rose's robust development.

When Rose was two, Laura learned that she was expecting another baby. Delighting in Rose, Almanzo and Laura eagerly anticipated another child. Would he be a boy? And would he be as bright as Rose? The baby was a boy—he looked just like Manly—but they never knew him well. Just two weeks after his birth one hot August day in 1889, the little boy died so quickly that the doctor came too late to even help. The little unnamed boy was buried atop the hill just west of town, the first of Laura's family to lie there. Many years later, Rose was questioned about her baby brother. It was a subject she could tell little about. "I know nothing about him," Rose wrote when she was 79, "because my mother wanted nothing said about it; I think she never stopped grieving and it was her way to be silent, and want silence about any unhappy subject."

But Rose did remember the fire. While Laura was still sick and numb with sorrow, a few days after the baby's death, Rose, trying to be helpful, fed the cookstove fire haysticks. She was competent at this task; it was nothing unusual, but that terrible day an accident occurred and within minutes the kitchen of the little gray house was ablaze. It was all that Laura could do to drag Rose and a few valuables out of the burning building. They had to watch it burn to the ground, for help was too far away and slow in coming. "I remember quite well," Rose recalled sadly, "watching the house burn and knowing that I had done it."

But who can say that the fire was Rose's fault? Stoves often exploded, and hot ashes frequently and dangerously puffed out of the tin pipes. Even Grandpa Ingalls came close to disaster one day in his little store downtown. Going down one Sunday morning to bank up the coals, the store stove blew up with a tremendous crash and although no damage occurred, Grandpa was thoroughly rattled himself. Fires were just another part of the hazard of living in pioneer days. Certainly Laura and Almanzo never dwelt on the house fire—they were too busy building another shanty to live in.

But their hearts were not in homesteading anymore. Dust blew, the sun burned and the land was barren. Through it all, compounded by worry, Manly's health grew worse and worse. He and Laura decided to try to stick it out on the homestead another year, but when no rain fell in the spring of 1890, they made new plans. Almanzo's parents had invited them to come to the fertile rolling hills of their farm in Minnesota. Almanzo could work when he felt like it, and there would be a bit of security for Manly, Laura and Rose. Comforting words and peaceful seasons on the Wilder farm worked like magic for Rose and her parents. But Manly's health still troubled him and after a year, they decided once again to seek relief elsewhere.

It was to Florida that the Wilders chose to go. "We want to see the world," Laura said and she tried to sound confident and happy. But really they wanted to see if Florida's climate would ease Manly's struggle with the effects of his stroke and the diphtheria. And so, the three Wilders traveled by train through the south and finally arrived at a little village deep in the whispering pines north of Pensacola. Rose heard the drawl of southern voices; she felt the hot, humid heat and she absorbed something of the dreamy, slowly moving Florida ways. This we know, for when she grew up she wrote about it.*

After a year in Florida, the Wilders decided to go home to Dakota. They traveled endless miles north and finally the train let them off at DeSmet. Grandma and Grandpa Ingalls and the aunts were delighted that the Wilders were home again, but the prairie had not yet released its grip of drought, which meant hard times for farmers and towns-

---

*When she grew up Rose wrote a story which she considered her very best: "Innocence." Its setting was the dreamy southern Florida area she remembered as a four-year old. The story dealt with the marriage of her mother's cousin Peter to a southern backwoods girl in the piney woods.

men alike. Almanzo decided to become one of the latter. He rented a little house not far from Laura's parents' and while Laura sewed for a dollar a day, he worked wherever he could. And Rose went to school.

Rose had learned to read at three, from sheer curiosity. She had learned the letters from a little ABC book by "asking and being told to stop asking." She had first read when she had noticed the printing on the cook-stove. "P A T." it said. "P A T, what's that?" Rose asked her father. Almanzo replied, "Pat." When Rose asked who Pat was, Almanzo told her he was Pat Murphy. She wrestled with that; she felt a definite discrepancy between those three letters and something as long as Pat Murphy. She could not cope with that mystery, but from that moment on, she could read.

While Rose's mind was growing and developing, Laura and Almanzo struggled for their daily bread. Almanzo worked wherever he could and daily Laura sewed at the dressmaker's. With both parents working, Rose was allowed to enter the DeSmet school at age five. Six was the age of admittance, but since Rose's Grandpa Ingalls was the town patriarch and on the school board, his granddaughter was allowed to enter a year in advance. From the kindergarten primer, Rose learned to write and she became so intensely fascinated with copying and writing words of her own that she developed what was called "writer's cramp" and had to be taken from school. "I wonder what it really was, "Rose mused seventy years later, "that nearly deprived me the use of a right arm."

Life in DeSmet was secure and safe for Rose and her parents during those hot, dry years in the early nineties, except for the fact that Almanzo and Laura were earning little more than enough to exist on. But Rose could walk down the long board sidewalks, where grasshoppers chirped, to her grandparents' home. The Ingalls home was a cozy, gray house, not empty and echoing like the rented house Rose lived in. In the parlor blind Aunt Mary sat in her rocking chair and showed Rose how to sew rag carpets. Grandma Ingalls taught Rose how to knit, and Grandpa made

Rose her very own footstool. A visit to Grandma's might also mean a special cup of cambric tea when Rose was good, and if she was very good, a cinnamon stick from the kitchen cupboard.

Sometimes Rose walked the other direction up Third Street and stopped to visit Mrs. Sherwood and her sister Genevieve. On the hot summer afternoons they sometimes sent Rose to the far-off ice cream parlor for ten cents worth of ice cream. "I hope . . . that ice cream still tastes as good to youngsters (in DeSmet) in the hot summers as it did to me," Rose wrote in 1968.

In 1894, when Rose was seven, she heard her parents talking of the "Land of the Big Red Apple." It was far-away — in Mansfield, Missouri, way down in the Ozark Mountains. When summer-time came, they were going there. Rose's prairie prelude was coming to a close.

II. THE OZARK YEARS

The Wilders—Laura, Manly and Rose—had little more than their courage to take with them when they said good-by that July morning and left DeSmet. The covered wagon carried all their worldly goods—a featherbed, quilts, small homemade cupboard, dishes and Laura's little lap desk. That special desk held the key to their future in Missouri, a single hundred dollar bill which Laura had carefully hoarded from her earnings at the dressmaker's shop. Rose knew about the money, but of course she was never to say anything about it.

Traveling with the Wilders to Missouri was another De-Smet family, the Cooley's. The two Cooley boys, Paul and George were Rose's playmates as they traveled the long road south from the dry Dakota prairie. Rose watched the countryside passing them by with her usual interest.* She vividly recalled her last look at South Dakota, the state of her birth . . .

> We reached the Missouri at Yankton (Rose wrote in 1935), in a string of covered wagons. The ferryman took them, one by one, across the wide yellow river. I sat between my parents in the wagon on the river bank, anxiously hoping to get across before dark . . . Looking around the edge of the wagon cover, I saw the whole earth billowing behind us to the sky. There was something savage and terrifying in that howling yellow swallowing the sky. The color came, I now suppose, from the sunset.
> "Well, that's our last sight of Dakota," my mother said.

Through the long summer days, the Wilders crossed Nebraska and Kansas. Rose found the trip infinitely interesting—the towns, cities, creeks and rivers and people all held a fascination for her—but her parents were weary and worried. Once Rose even forced Paul Cooley to let her drive the Cooley team a whole mile! That was a guilty secret which Rose did not break for seventy years. And then, at long last, they reached the Ozark hills.

It was strange not to hear the wind blow any more. But once in Missouri, looking far off into the blue hills and driving through the cool oak woods, a sense of home came over the Wilders. On the last day of August, the covered wagon rolled into the little mountain town of Mansfield. "This is where we stop," Rose heard her mother say.

Once they arrived in Mansfield, things moved quickly. Almanzo looked and looked for a piece of land to buy. The farms he saw were mostly rocky hills, with oak woods scattered up and down the ridges. He and Laura both realized that farming in Missouri would be much different than farm-

---

*Laura recorded all they saw and experienced in a little diary. This diary may be seen at the Museum at Mansfield, Mo., and Rose's account of their life after arriving in Missouri, may be read in **On The Way Home.**

ing in Dakota. But finally they found a rough, rocky piece of land that suited them both. It came complete with a log cabin, fruit trees, a spring and a mortgage. These things Rose learned as they packed up the wagon for the last time and drove out to the farm her mother had christened "Rocky Ridge."

That first winter on Rocky Ridge was spent in the windowless log cabin right on the edge of the deep, rocky ravine where the creek flowed. Almanzo and Laura worked hard, clearing the land, and for fifty cents a load Almanzo sold firewood in town. Rose said that the first wagonload of wood sold was the turning point; from then on, through hard work and luck, life on Rocky Ridge Farm became increasingly happier for them.

Of course Rose went to school in Mansfield—as soon as they were settled, she walked off each morning to class. It was not long before Almanzo and Laura had bought Rose her own donkey to ride. Truth to tell, Rose hated her Spookendyke, who was she said, "a stubborn, fat little beast who liked to slump his ears and neck and shoulders suddenly when going downhill and tumble me off his head." Usually, Rose and Spookendyke walked side by side over the hills and if Rose was lucky, they arrived at the same time.

A day at the red-brick school in Mansfield was often long and dull for Rose—she was too smart to be interested in the book full of things like this:

Exercise in verbs. Insert the words in following sentences:

The dog _ _ _ _ _ _ _ _ _ _ _ at the cat.
The horse _ _ _ _ _ _ _ _ _ _ _ the wagon.

Even Rose's mother agreed that the work was silly. She could understand why Rose often sat daydreaming the hours away in school. Sometimes when she had quickly finished her lessons, Rose looked at the professor . . . "The Professor used to sit before us," Rose remembered, "tipped back in his chair, watching us study, ready to catch us if

—9—

we whispered. He did not have any desk; he kept his chewing tobacco in his pocket. In one hand he held a long cane —it was intended to represent authority but he usually used it to scratch his back."

Lunch was perhaps the most interesting part of the day for Rose. Then she could read. There were two shelves of books "donated" to the school and every day Rose picked a book and took her lunch pail away from the others and read. So started her life-long quest for knowledge and her eager devouring of books, words and ideas. Rose even had her own language—Fispooko—which she had invented with nouns and verbs and prepositions and all, and she used to talk it to Spookendyke on the trips to and from school.

The evenings at home in the log cabin were cozy and comfortable. There, Rose said, "nothing to worry or hurt us till tomorrow and Mama was reading. That was best of all." One by one, Laura read all the books aloud from the school library.

When spring came, Rose helped to put in the first crop on the newly cleared hills. All summer long, Rose ran and played and explored the rocky hills and gentle valleys. She picked wild berries, sometime to sell in town, sometimes to bake in a pie. With her mother, she played in the little creek just below the cabin and they tamed wild birds and squirrels. And once Rose even ventured alone into Williams Cave—nearly a mile underground, until she came to a great dark lake and waded in it up to her arm-pits. Then Rose's torch went out; she pondered a bit—and came out.

A year went by and then another. Rocky Ridge Farm was thriving and Rose was ten. The hens were laying, the fruit trees were growing and the garden was doing well. Now, when Rose went to school, her books were new and her dresses were as nice as the ones the town girls wore. But first impressions stayed . . . Rose Wilder was a country girl, and at first she had been a poor country girl. Town girls didn't forget that. And besides that, Rose Wilder was smart. She always beat everyone in the Friday spell-downs.

Rose herself was too shy, too proud, to break down the barriers. As she said, there were no invitations to parties; she was left out.

The Wilders no longer lived in a log cabin — it was Laura's and Almanzo's dream to build a fine, big house from materials from the farm. Their first triumph was a little frame house under the spreading oaks on the edge of the ravine. They lived there a bit and all of a sudden, Rose became a "town girl." Her parents decided to move into Mansfield for a while, so that Almanzo could work as a drayman and deliver fuel oil. Laura, too, found opportunities to earn—she cooked for the railroad men and boarded the banker. Whenever they could, Manly and Laura went out to Rocky Ridge to work.

During the summer of 1898, the Wilders of Mansfield had visitors in their little house on the edge of Mansfield. Rose's Grandpa and Grandma Wilder, along with her Aunt Laura, stopped to make a long visit. They were on their way to Louisiana to settle down near Eliza Jane and Perley. The Wilder house must have been full to overflow—and having two Lauras around confused everyone. It was then that Rose decided to have her mother called Bess, from her middle name Elizabeth. And so Manly started calling his Laura Bess or Bessie. And from that point on Rose called her mother nothing but Mama Bess.

Rose's education was unusual, to say the least. Soon after she came to town to live, a family moved to Mansfield with a whole wall of books. The friendly owners let Rose borrow each one. One by one she read all the English novelists and playwrights; histories and poems and romances. Rose reveled in each one. She even began to dream about becoming a writer herself — even though it might mean abandoning her dream of becoming Rose Wilder, Famous Artist and designer of monograms. Life as a Jo March, spinster authoress seemed fine to Rose now.

Usually, Rose was not going to school, because she was "mad at the teacher." Year after year, Mansfield found teachers who were no match of the spirited inquisitiveness

OR the intelligence of Rose Wilder. One first day of school, the hapless teacher assigned Rose's class an exercise in transposition—they were to interpret lines of Tennyson. When Rose was asked for her work, she declared that poetry could not be transposed; what it said was not what it meant. Then the teacher turned to listen to Charlie Day's feeble attempt, which he praised. This Rose might have borne, but Teacher turned to her and said, "Let this be a lesson to you, Miss Wilder; you fail because you do not try . . . If at first you do not succeed, you must not weakly give up; you must . . ."

Here Rose stood up, slammed her books, and said in fury, "I will not stay here and listen to such stupid, stupid . . . "—and went home.

At home, up in the hayloft of the barn, Rose spent day after day eating apples while she devoured the algebra and geometry books , studied Physiology and Latin and daydreamed about life beyond the Ozark hills.

The summer of 1903 brought Aunt Eliza Jane and cousin Wilder for a visit to Mansfield. They lived in Crowley, Louisiana, where there was a High School. At the end of the summer, Rose, Papa and Mama Bess and Aunt E. J. had all decided that Rose should go to Crowley and try the High School there.

For the first time, Rose was on her own—almost. Of course she lived with her aunt and cousin and Grandma Wilder was nearby and so were Uncle Perley and the cousins, but for the first time, Rose found a school where she could learn the way she wanted to. And they offered Latin. Rose had no schooling to show on a record, but she passed the entrance examination with her self-education. Of Latin she knew nothing and it was required in order to graduate, but Rose was thrilled with the prospect of learning the three years' worth in the single year she would be in Crowley. This she did—coming out on top of her class of seven in Latin. At graduation exercises, in a white lace dress, Rose read her very own Latin poem. So ended her topsy-turvy educational career.

Rose was seventeen. Her schooling was done—of that she was sure. What was there for her to do? Mansfield was out of the question. She loved Mama Bess and Papa dearly, but life there held no challenge as far as she was concerned. She knew that beyond the blue hills there lay cities, opportunities and chances for a young, ambitious girl to make her mark. But that was a problem—being a girl. No "nice" girl went out on her own anywhere; no father wanted his daughter to work for a living and no mother wanted her girl talked about. But still, with infinite patience and understanding, Laura and Almanzo Wilder let Rose go. She had learned telegraphy from Mr. Burney in Mansfield and she was determined to use her skill to make her living. And so, Rose left home. Kansas City was her first stop and Western Union was her first employer. Rose was on her own.

III. CAREER GIRL

In Kansas City Rose Wilder, the girl from the Ozarks quickly was transformed by the big city and the thrill of being an independent self-supporting "bachelor girl." True, ministers shook their heads from the pulpit when they preached against this new breed of woman; true grandmothers were shocked and parents were worried, but Rose and the legion of young girls like her sailed on in their battle for "woman's rights." Clothes had to be servicable for work-ing—Rose naturally shortened her skirts so that they actually cleared the dirty Kansas City sidewalks. "From man's very back," Rose recalled, "we stole the shirt." And when Rose cut her long tresses and wore her hair in a smart, short style, Mansfield gasped when she appeared home on a visit.

Rose's boundless energy and enthusiasm for her career prompted her to work double shifts at the telegrapher's key. Each day, from the Main Office she rushed to the Midland Hotel to take over the night shift. Her wages were $60 per month and as Rose said, she was "riding on top of the world." Then one day Rose got wind that all Western Union girls who did not type would be fired the next day. Rose wasn't daunted—she just went home from her 16 hour day and stayed up all night to master the use of the typewriter.

Kansas City was just the first stop for Rose in her telegrapher's career. There she had made her mark by participating in the first operator's strike, but it was not long until Rose Wilder was manager of Western Union's office in Mount Vernon, Indiana and in a long succession of other towns and cities scattered all over the country. Finally, in 1908, she had landed in San Francisco.

San Francisco was a glorious spot to live, but Rose was growing bored with the telegrapher's life. She learned that real estate was booming in California and she was determined to try her hand at selling it. And so one day Miss Rose Wilder presented herself at the firm of Stine & Kendrick and offered her talents and services as a land salesman. Only through persuasion did Rose wrangle a job, thus making her the very first female real estate salesperson in California. The other men on the firm were wary; they fought her bitterly—and later Rose even learned that sometimes her fellow workers would throw a sale over to a rival firm rather than let it go to Rose! Little wonder that Rose was an active suffragist.

One fellow employee at Stine and Kendrick was not so hostile to Rose. His name was Gillette Lane and although several men had begged Rose to marry them before, when Gillette asked, she said yes. So, on March 24, 1909, when she was twenty-three, Rose Wilder became Mrs. Gillette Lane. And because of the booming real estate sales they were making, the new Mr. and Mrs. Lane were able to take a grand honeymoon. They stopped to visit Papa and Mama Bess in Missouri of course, and then they went on to New York City where they had the awesome experience of staying at the Waldorf Astoria Hotel.

Gillette was jolly, personable, likable, amusing, a dreamer and schemer and completely in accord with Rose's ideas about a woman's place in the world. She liked that. From the beginning, Rose and Gillette agreed that theirs would be a partnership of two; Rose would be no parasite—she would carry an equal load in the matter of making a living. For a short while Rose tried being a housewife, but the experience made her so unhappy that Gillette said with understanding that "I know you must have work or I'll lose you." And so Rose went back to real estate.

Eventually, Rose was responsible for the sale of over a million dollars of land in the San Fernando Valley—much of it, old Spanish-grant land being parceled for fruit and poultry farms. She and Gillette lived a happy, carefree life —they owned a car; Rose drove of course; they traveled, made friends and made money, until World War I broke out in Europe. Then farmers became scared, ceased all land-buying and the real estate business folded. This meant a new beginning for Rose, an ending for Gillette, and the beginning of the end for them both.

Rose and Gillette were in Napa when six saleless months hit them. Finally, they moved back to San Francisco and sought out new means of livelihood. Rose was lucky—a young friend, Bessie Beatty was writing the woman's page for the San Francisco **Bulletin** and she helped Rose get a few free-lance pieces published in the paper. The staff took notice at what "Rose Wilder Lane" was sending in; soon she was asked to join the staff, under the watchful eye of editor Fremont Older.

For Rose, writing was a dizzying and glamourous occupation. As Bessie Beatty's editorial assistant, she was to concoct light, romantic serials for the **Bulletin's** feminine audience. But the day soon came when Mr. Older summoned Rose. She expected a quick dismissal, but instead, the great titan of old-time west-coast editors challenged Rose.

"You can do better than the things you're turning out," he suggested.

"You wouldn't print better stuff," Rose answered. "If Victor Hugo came in with the manuscript for **Les Miserables,** you'd refuse it."

"I'd print every word . . ." Mr. Older assured her.

From that time on, the **Bulletin** got the best Rose Lane could write.

From trashy love sagas, Rose started writing features on interesting San Francisco people and places. It was a grand time to find material, for the "city by the bay" was preparing for the 1915 Panama-Pacific International Exposition. One of Rose's first triumphs was a series she wrote called "The Story of Art Smith." Since aviation was new and featured heavily at the Fair (Rose had flown, strapped to the wing of an airplane, over San Francisco Bay)—Rose's story of the daring aviation feats of Art Smith were very popular. Later, the stories were published in book form.*

Rose was becoming known all over California. She covered important stories, like the San Francisco water project and then she did a timely series of interviews with prune and apricot growers she met while walking through the Santa Clara Valley.

As soon as she could plan for it, Rose longed to bring her parents out to California from Rocky Ridge Farm in Missouri. The plan materialized somewhat when, in the summer of 1915, Mama Bess was able to come for an extended visit with Rose and Gillette. It was a time they remembered always, and now readers can share their joy in the letters Laura wrote home to Almanzo, now published in **West From Home.**

As Rose's career extended and grew, Gillette's struggles for a job mounted. He combed San Francisco for work, but usually unable to find more than a few days work here and there. Although he was often discouraged and impractical, he never lost his zest—even if it was misguided. One December fifth, he spent his last money on dozens of red roses for Rose's birthday—when there was no money for food in the house. Rose had to rush out in the street when she got

---

*The slim paperback volume on Art Smith is highly valued by aviation collectors as well as collector of Rose's works. It is most rare and difficult to locate in any of the several different editions which were printed.

home from work and sell flowers for a "charity"—in order to gather enough funds for supper!

Despite efforts by both Gillette and Rose, they were growing apart. Rose was now writing for **Sunset Magazine,** free-lancing stories and articles and becoming a household name in California and beyond. In 1917, her first major book appeared, a biography—the first ever written of Henry Ford. As Rose's success continued to climb, life with Gillette continued to be difficult. Finally, they decided to part. In 1918, they were divorced. Their rosy hopes and plans of nine years earlier were dashed. Perhaps they were ahead of their times, perhaps they were incompatible because success came to the wrong mate. But Rose never elaborated on the failure of her marriage. One day, many years later, she opened the newspaper to read that Gillette was dead. She called her memories "poignant" of the "two happy but profoundly lost and bewildered lovers who died a quarter of a century ago."

Now, although single again, as she would remain the rest of her life, Rose's life was filled with work and a goodly number of friends. One of them was Berta Hoerner, a young artist; another was Jack London, whose story Rose wrote splendidly for **Sunset Magazine** in 1917. Her circle of California friends included many just-about-famous persons in the arts. One friend likened them all to the zestful, fun-loving, creative "Bohemians"—but he added that Rose and her group were nothing like present day "hippies." Rose herself was "a wonderful character, such as one meets only in a thousand."

Professionally, Rose was reaching always higher heights. Soon after her divorce from Gillette, her first novel was published—**Diverging Roads.** The book, fiction, of course in its appearance, was the thinly disguised tale of her own marriage and its ultimate failure. Mama Bess didn't like it much, but at least Rose could now add novelist to her list of credentials which included biographer, reporter and feature writer. Even though she was comfortable and had made a niche for herself in west-coast writing, Rose was restless. Later, she attributed her feelings to the war. Before the Armistice was even signed and World War I ended, Rose and Berta Hoerner had closed up business in California and had settled themselves in a house in Greenwich Village. They both felt that New York City might open some opportunities to them in their respective careers of author and artist.

In New York, Rose's literary talents quickly found outlets in such magazines as **Ladies' Home Journal, Good Housekeeping** and **Pictorial Review.** During this period, Rose ghostwrote a best-selling book for Frederick O'Brien: **White Shadows on the South Seas.** When the book became such a huge success (it even became an early movie), Rose was anxious to claim her rightful credit and O'Brien was just as anxious to call the book his own. The controversy surrounding this volume was never settled. Rose was busy, too, consulting with Herbert Hoover, who became her personal friend. Hoover was then a prominent figure because of his relief work following the war, and it was Rose Wilder Lane who told his story in her second biography, **The Making of Herbert Hoover.**

Berta Hoerner, Rose's roommate married artist Elmer Hader not long after arriving in New York and then Rose moved to Croton-on-the-Hudson. Her new friends in New York were among the brightest and most promising writers and artists, among them were Floyd Dell, the author and Socialist. Many of the bright young thinkers with whom Rose associated were being excited and involved with the Communist party. Rose went to the meetings, she engaged in stimulating discussions and although she did not become a party member, she was a thoroughly convinced Communist. She felt that Communism was a correct interpretation of American ideals. But before she had time to become actively involved in the American Communist Party, the American Red Cross and the Near East Relief offered her a challenging job: they asked that Rose travel abroad in war-torn Europe and Asia investigating and reporting on conditions for the American press. Rose, of course said yes. After all she was a pioneer by birth and by ancestry. Travel was in her blood and the years ahead would hold as many adventures as any pioneer had faced traveling across the West!

IV. AN AMERICAN IN FOREIGN LANDS

As soon as passage could be arranged, Rose sailed for France. Her first post was in the Red Cross offices in Paris, where she sent "sob stuff" to the American magazines and papers. The Red Cross had assigned Rose to write effectively about the problems of refugees, of bombed cities and hungry orphans in hopes that this publicity would prompt generous Americans to continue financing relief work abroad. And so most of Rose's writings which she dispatched to American magazines and papers through her New York agents dealt with what she saw among the war-made unfortunates. "I wrote . . . about those victims of war," Rose remembered, in such a way, "that should have wrung dollars from the stoniest American pocketbook."

After a brief time in Paris, where she developed a close friendship with writer Dorothy Thompson, Rose traveled rapidly through Europe and then into the Near East. The dates and places refuse to arrange themselves in any order. But she saw Greece, Italy, Russia, Yugoslavia, and made excursions into Egypt, Arabia, Armenia, Perisa, and many other foreign lands and ports. At home, Laura and Almanzo were often worried, and so was Rose's old Grandma Ingalls far-off in DeSmet. But she never failed to write them and assure the home-folks. In a letter to Ma Ingalls, Laura assured her that Rose said "not to worry, because they are treated like visiting princesses."

Rose's incredible adventures could fill several volumes, but perhaps most important for her, she saw first hand what Communism really was. One by one, she saw the Red Army prey upon poor, sick and starving war victims and their countries. Any inclination she may have once felt towards that form of government was quickly forgotten by Rose. She did, however, find her Marxist knowledge of advantage when she was arrested a few times by the Cheka—it made her quick release possible!

While connected with the Near East Relief, Rose traveled with her friend Helen Boylston, called "Troub." Quite by chance, the two women came to the ancient, beautiful little country of Albania. Those mountains, the independent, unique people who lived there and their brave spirits immediately appealed to Rose. She fell in love with the little nation and spent as much time there as she could. In numerous, dangerous expeditions into the northern highlands, Rose was the first foreign woman the natives had ever seen. She knew that when her other duties were over, she would come back to Albania.

Although she traveled tirelessly and widely through all of Europe with the Red Cross and Near East Relief, Rose never neglected her career on the home front. Sometimes, writing with typewriter on her knees, wrapped in sheepskin and speeding in a box-car when it was forty below outside, Rose wrote. She dispatched countless articles to American magazines like the **National Geographic, Harper's, World's Traveler** and **Ladies Home Journal.** For a time she was foreign correspondent for the Minneapolis **Journal.** And while abroad she sent two books home for Harper and Brothers to publish: **The Dancer of Shamakha,** which she translated from the French and **The Peaks of Shala,** a wonderful volume which did much to inform the Americans about Albania. And while absent in Europe, Rose won the second O. Henry Prize for the best short story of 1922: "Innocence." From afar, Rose was building her reputation as one of America's best penwomen

Finally, at long last, Rose decided to come home. Home, this time, was Rocky Ridge Farm and Mama Bess and Papa. Rose reached Mansfield in early 1924. After a rest in the old home, she set up her typewriter once again in her upstairs bedroom and started to write. Now, she turned to Ozark life and customs for her material. Troub—Helen Boylston professionally, had come back to Rocky Ridge with Rose and together the two roamed the hills and valleys looking for tales and information for Rose to use. First Rose wrote **Cindy: A Romance of the Ozarks;** next she did a novel called **Hill-Billy,** based roughly on her friend in Mansfield, N. J. Craig. Rose also took time out to write a masterful novel based on her friend Jack London's life—she called it **He Was A Man.**

Wilder Home Association
Mansfield, Mo.

Rose and her donkey, Spookendyke.

Rose (behind flag, fourth from left), posed with Sunday School before leaving De Smet in 1894.

Laura greets Rose at the rock house on the farm which Rose had built in 1928.

Rocky Ridge Farmhouse, a place Rose always called home. She returned there to live and visit periodically until her mother's death, in 1957.

Rose's home at 23 King Street near Danbury. This picture shows it soon after she bought the house in 1938. Later she remodeled and improved it continuously over the years.

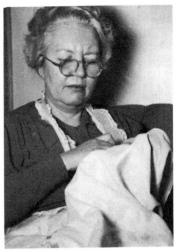

New York, 1920's.

Rose's interest in needlework led her to write two magazine series and a book on the subject, plus a lifetime hobby of creating beautiful handwork herself.

Rose's desk and some of her books in her study at Danbury. Today her various desks and typewriters are displayed in Mansfield and DeSmet. Her ten thousand volume library is now in Virginia.

1924   **1930's**

1940's   **1961**

And between books, Rose's short stories and pointed articles were gobbled up by the top magazines of the day. When she wrote for a magazine, her name got top billing on the cover. When she sent a story to her agents, they demanded top price for the tale.

Rose loved being among the hills again. She had really been away from home almost fifteen years and during that time, her parents built up the farm to a place of comfort, beauty and prosperity. And now that she was able, Rose provided her parents with every luxury they could want. She bought them their first car; she took Laura and Troub out to California; she bought Almanzo fine horses. The three years Rose spent at home were a rejuvination from her hectic years abroad and a time to enjoy her wonderful parents and their home in the beautiful hills.

But once again Europe, particularly Albania, beckoned. At home, Rose had a modern home built of rock constructed for Laura and Almanzo; she thought they might like a change —and then she and Helen Boylston sailed across the Atlantic. They stopped in Paris, where they bought a 1927 Ford, and proceeded to drive down through Italy and eventually settle in Albania. Everywhere they went, people gasped. First: "The new model Ford!" Second: "Three women alone!!!" Women who drove alone were curosities in those days in Europe.

In the capitol city of Albania, Tirana, Rose and Troub and their maid settled in an impressive domicile, complete with a native **Kavass,** who cooked, cleaned, escorted, marketed, carried water, and "thanked the good God for this opportunity to be in our household, and asks only to remain with us forever, to live and die in our service."* His salary was $5.50 per month.

Rose had a wonderful affinity for the Albanians and their way of life; she became nothing short of a national heroine of the country and remains so to this day. She was personal friend of King Zog—he even begged for her hand in marriage. But Zog was a Moselm, and Rose suspected

*Letters from Rose to "Darlings" (Papa and Mama Bess), from Tirana.

that she might be compelled to share the King with several other wives, so she declined the honor. She did fall in love with a young orphan boy named Rexh Meta, who once saved her life on a bleak monutainside. Rexh (pronounced Redge) was just like Rose's son and eventually she educated him at Oxford in England.

Although faraway and even isolated from the modern world, Rose was continually in front of the American eye as her name as a writer soared. At this time, Rose Wilder Lane was reputed to be the highest paid female writer on the American scene. It was an ideal situation—living in a country she loved and writing for her native country, but nevertheless, Rose was an American and an American pioneer as well. After several blissful years abroad, Rose was lured home again to Rocky Ridge. Once more she went "along smooth trails" (an Albanian expression) back home to Missouri.

Rose's situation to live in Mansfield must have surprised many of her worldly friends, but it was nothing but natural to Rose. She had seen most of the world, but Rocky Ridge always seemed to beckon. Back in Missouri, Rose felt a true sense of home. Her parents were living in the stone cottage across the ridge from the old farmhouse and Rose settled down there (after modernizing the house) to write. She entertained often; friends from the East, Dorothy Thompson, Troub, Catherine Brody and other authors were always popping in to visit the Ozarks. Rose joined her mother's Mansfield club, the Justamere Club and the ladies were frequently asked out to Rocky Ridge. And every so often, Rose invited starry-eyed young journalists and reporters from the Springfield newspapers for a weekend on Rocky Ridge. The housekeeper cooked delicious Ozark-style meals, but the feast was really Rose's monologues after supper. Gathered around the big rock fireplace, Rose spellbound her visitors with her tales, her opinions and her theories of writing.

In the early 1930's, when the Depression had reached deep into the Ozark hills with a vengeance, Rose thought a long while, back to the depression she and her parents had lived through, in 1893. Then, nobody came in to organize work camps, or to tell the banks what to do, or made weak people weaker by giving them what they could earn. She remembered picking berries for ten cents a gallon; that thought would horrify people in 1931. But why? Rose could not understand, but she could demonstrate with her pen. She would write a reply to pessimists, and show that hard times could always be won over to always better times, if people could hope, wait and work. Her message came in the form of **Let the Hurricane Roar.**

Let the Hurricane Roar was published in 1933, during President Roosevelt's "bank holiday." On the surface, it was a touching romance of two Dakota pioneers who struggled and perservered against the elements, and through hard times, struggled with independence and pride. Depression-shocked people loved the book, and Rose knew that the underlying message it carried was the reason why. **Hurricane** became the top best-seller of 1933 and 1934. The **Saturday Evening Post** serialized it and **Country Gentleman** did likewise, not once, but twice. Whether she knew it or not at the time, Rose had acquired a particular image. She was now the prairie penwoman of the 1930's . . .

V. PIONEER STORIES, PIONEER PRINCIPLES

The wonderful success of **Hurricane,** because of its subtle message that individualistic, pioneer American spirit, convinced Rose that this theme might serve her well in setting forth literature which would help convince Americans that no Depression could conquer them. At Rocky Ridge in Missouri, Rose worked steadily and continually on short stories and articles for her usual leading markets, and more often than not, they revolved around the pioneers. Rose always seemed to write about what she knew and loved best: Albania, the Ozarks, . . . and pioneering was her own heritage. From her own deep well of memory as a prairie child and from the stores of memories she borrowed from her mother and father,

Rose wrote of the settlement and homesteading days in Dakota fifty years earlier.

Most of Rose's best stories were published by the **Saturday Evening Post** during the 1930's and her name was usually billed Number One. The tales often dealt with blizzards, crop failures and everyday joys and sorrows of the homesteader. Some of the story lines are easy to trace back to actual events in the Ingalls and Wilder family stories. Names like Perley, Eliza Jane, Charles and Caroline were Rose's characters; places like Burr Oak, The Big Woods, and Malone were locales Rose alluded to.

In the midst of Rose's activity and career, she understood a shy little desire on her mother's part to write, too. Mama Bess was past sixty and for years she had written for local farm papers and magazines. But her mind traveled back to her own girlhood on the prairie and particularly to her wonderful father—Rose's Grandpa Ingalls, now long dead. Mama Bess wanted more than anything to preserve some of her Pa's stories and capture something of his wit and character for boys and girls. Rose of course was eager to help.

Laura Wilder was largely untrained in writing, but her talent for expression and great feeling for interpretation were natural gifts. That Rose could sense. She knew that she, the professional, the "name" in the family, only need give her mother some direction and "push" and her mother could be on her own as a writer. After several years of work and suggestions, and a couple of well-directed pushes (some by Rose's dear friends the Haders, by then nationally-known children's book creators) — Laura Ingalls Wilder's first book, **Little House in the Big Woods,** was published. It was an immediate success, much to Laura's surprise, and all she could do was continue the long saga of her childhood for eager readers. And so Rose found herself lovingly directing her mother in small ways, as well as continuing her own mounting career, through all eight of Laura's "Little House" books.

For one as prolific as Rose was during the 1930's, it is odd to know that she considered writing "drudgery"!

Once she confided to a reporter that the only thing that compelled her to sit down at the typewriter was the state of her bank-book balance. But she certainly didn't crave wealth, and she cared little for fame. Shortly after she signed a royalty check for $30,000 for one story, she did an article for a mere $150 because the topic interested her. And another time she contracted for a story from an editor's orders, but she hated the subject. When the words just would not flow together in the usual realistic Lane style, Rose gave up the half-hearted job and returned the check. But when she believed in a subject, or felt caught up in it, an editor could expect a book in five or six weeks. For years, Rose's usual reaction after completing a manuscript was that she would never write another line. But finally, that feeling left her. "It's happened too many times," Rose explained, "to frighten me again."

In her style and careful choice of words, Rose was a true craftsman of words. She did all her composition on her faithful Underwood;* she said she couldn't THINK in longhand. She rough-drafted all her work on cheap yellow typewriter paper and she worked and re-worked her material until the style was "just-so." It was Rose's policy to go to great pains to make her thoughts and ideas crystal-clear, with no ambiguity, and her finished drafts were universally admired for their brilliance.

While writing of the plains of her birth, Rose also turned back to the town of her childhood for a delightful series of tales for the **Saturday Evening Post.** The little, turn of the century town was easily seen as Mansfield and the young girl of each story, Ernestine, was of course Rose. The delicious stories of small town life, scandal, thwarted love and growing up were popular all over the nation, but of course it was in Mansfield that people rushed to scan the latest **Post** for local names or references. For a time, it seemed that all Mansfield was peeved with Rose—either slighted because they had been left out of a story, or angry (usually feigned anger!) that they had been exposed! The

---

*The Underwood she bought in Springfield, Mo. for $15.00—a used one and in the 1960's she told me she was still using it. I.V.L.

Ernestine series was collected in 1935 and published as **Old Home Town** and though it was fairly recent history when published, it is pure nostalgia today.

In 1936, Rose reached fifty and that full, thinking half-century had made her a woman of extraordinary wisdom. More than ever, Rose "looked at America." She pondered over the changes she had seen. When she traveled, she made a point to talk to people—all sorts of people: shop-girls, grocers, politicians, teachers and boys who pumped gas. With a mature, adult patriotism, Rose Lane loved America and regarded its democratic way of life as the last hope for the world. Her long years of life abroad and at home had crystalized her thinking into that of a fundamentalist American. She believed passionately in the tenets on which America had been formed. Through her writings, in her associations and by example, Rose celebrated and stressed **Individualism,** the basic right of every human being to control his or her destiny.

Rose's explosive thesis on personal liberty truly burst out in a flame of new and clarified ideas with her sensational **Saturday Evening Post** article, "Credo.' That piece began with the rather startling statement that "In 1919, I was a Communist . . ." And then, in her own magnificent style, Rose stated the essence of her beliefs: anti-communism, inferentially anti-New Deal (though not mentioning politics) and wholly Individualist thought. The amazing reader-response stunned everyone at the **Post** offices; for more than a week most of the **Post's** mail bags contained letters applauding that article. Rose's friend and editor of the **Post,** George Lorimer, confided that in all his experience he had never seen such reader response—"Credo" was undoubtedly the most successful magazine story ever published in the United States. Rose herself received three thousand letters, which thrilled her and convinced her that grassroots America wholeheartedly agreed that American values and individualist thought were the backbone of the United States. "Credo" was rushed into print as a small book entitled **Give Me Liberty** and for twenty or more years the book kept being reprinted and cherished by thousands of Americans.

Rose's next book, **Free Land** was another statement of her principles. Essentially, this novel was a plot she had used before: a young couple homesteading in the Dakotas. But **Free Land** was written because Rose was mad; she was tired of hearing people whine that "everything is changed now; there's no more free land." (the government had repealed the homestead act in 1935) "Everything certainly is changed now," Rose agreed, but "as to any 'free' land, there never was any." The dramatic light in which Rose portrayed the courageous Dakotans sought to show that the "free" land was won with sacrifice and endless toil of the generation just passed. The public loved **Free Land.** Soon it was Number One on the best seller lists. The **Post** serialized it. Just as Helen Hayes had adapted **Let the Hurricane Roar** for radio, **Free Land** also became a radio drama. As a writer, Rose Wilder Lane had reached another glittering success.

Rose wrote **Free Land** in the apartment she had taken in New York City. Her parents had moved back to the farmhouse on Rocky Ridge and Rose decided to settle back in the East. There, soon after **Free Land** appeared, she had the unique experience to mingle with South Dakotans at a meeting of that state's society in New York City. It was a first for Rose. "Until the day of this dinner, I have not known or seen any South Dakotans," Rose remarked in her speech to the group. She spoke with pleasure of the response to **Free Land** by South Dakotans. "I have received hundreds of letters," she said, and "It was wonderful to know that the people of South Dakota are so completely versed in the history of their state."

Though Rose was a famous and frequently lionized authoress, she considered herself a "typical middle-class, middle-western, middle-aged person, with simple tastes." But to many she was considered the most amazing individual ever met. Young people graviatated to Rose and she was their champion. In the darkest Depression days back in the Ozarks, Rose had housed and educated the two Turner boys from Douglas County; she sent John through the University of Missouri and he was just one of many students whose education was financed by Rose's generosity. Another favorite was Norma

Lee Browning, who Rose met while doing research for **Free Land** at the University of Missouri. Norma says that Rose taught her the groundworks of writing (she became nationally-known columnist and author) besides which "I loved and adored and worshipped her."

Soon after **Free Land** appeared, Rose was told point-blank that she could increase her usual yearly $100,000 income if she would "go along" with the Communist trend of writing and court the Marxists who were in control of many of the big publishing houses. Such an idea Rose Lane abhorred. She lamented the disintegration of writing in the U.S. and she felt that the breed of great editors she had once known were gradually slipping away. "The older established authors with big names," Rose remarked " are shell-shocked from the depression year. They're writing—yes. Because they must. But what are they writing?" Because of such conditions her profession—in which she was a veteran—was losing its appeal. Despite the facts that two or three editors were hounding her for another novel and the magazine market was ever-ready for her work, Rose was tapering off in her career. She saw her mission as something much more important than more fame, more money and more popular acclaim.

VI. ROSE AND HER "ARMY OF PRINCIPLES"

In 1938, Rose bought a pleasant little farmhouse on rural King Street near Danbury, Connecticut and settled down there to live. Country life always was her forte, but for a time she maintained her apartment in New York where she could run in on business or dash off one of her less and less frequent articles. The King Street house was an immediate challenge to Rose—it needed remodeling. Her old love of homemaking prevailed and with her own startled muscles Rose built bookcases, poured cement, painted and recovered furniture. Outside, on her pleasantly situated three acres, she gardened and raised most of her own food.

Rose's willingness to write commercially was ever-dwindling, but soon after coming out to Danbury in 1938, Eilene Tighe came out to visit Rose and she enticed her to do writing for the new magazine she was editing, **Woman's Day.** Rose was immediately impressed with Eilene's editorial qualities and although **Woman's Day** could pay but $50 an article — Rose's asking price HAD been $1,500 — she started to regularly appear in that magazine. Many of her frequent, early articles dealt with her occupation at the moment—homemaking. With her usual homey style, Rose shared her experiences in remodeling the Danbury house, covering furniture, college-educating sons, and then came a series on American needlework. One story told about "My House in the Country," while another invited readers to "Come Into My Kitchen." "Back in the (late thirties and early forties) Rose recalled in 1964, "when the Communists blockade of American media was so solid that I couldn't say anything I wanted to say anywhere else— but in **Woman's Day."**

As war came to Europe again, bringing on its heels the Italian domination of Rose's beloved Albania, she was not writing to any great extent, but she was still most active. On the Danbury "farm" she raised much of her own food, she took time to continue her life-long hobby of creating beautiful needlework, she entertained many friends for short or extended periods and she corresponded extensively with her Mama Bess in Missouri about the last of the "Little House" books. The years since 1932, when her first book appeared, had brought Mama Bess great fame as a writer and through each book, Rose offered her wise counsel and assistance with expression and content.

Much of Rose's time was spent in study. She had always loved books, and the shelves in Danbury contained as many as 8,000 volumes. Through her reading, Rose had become an authority on government, economics, history, philosophy, religion and theory. This accumulated wisdom served her well when she wrote her most important and explosive book in 1942.

For years, Rose had been appalled at what she felt was a diminishing of American's personal rights through the New Deal programs. The very tenets of the foundation of this country were being trespassed upon, Rose felt. Her answer to this was a timely book which she wrote "at white heat." She called it **The Discovery of Freedom.**

Discovery's essence was that all societies before the Americans had been told what to do—by a priest, by a king, or some other authority—and that they had accepted it. The American discovery of course, was that rightly, each human being is free and should be allowed to conduct his or her life. "Freedom means self-control, no more, no less," Rose stated. In her book she drew upon her vast store of knowledge for evidence of her thesis that the American way was the hope of the future. It has often been remarked that Rose Lane's **Discovery of Freedom** is to the idea of human freedom what Marx's **Das Kapital** is to the notion of socialism.

Peculiarly, the publishers of **Discovery** made no effort to promote the book. "The New York critics damned it," Rose remarked; perhaps one of the nicest things said about the work came from Mama Bess: "It is her best work and it is fascinating reading," she said. Of the small printing of the book, many copies were bought up and destroyed by Communists who saw ideas like Rose's dangerous threats to their ideas of socialism.

The Discovery of Freedom brought Rose no wealth—she returned the advanced royalty check—and hardly fame, but it was an enormous accomplishment; something intangible. "You started the modern literature of freedom in 1942 . . ." someone wrote Rose once, and it was true. Gradually, precious copies of **Discovery** circulated and whole lives were changed and new thinking and ideas poured into minds entrenched by New Deal policies and politics. Rose Wilder Lane became the "grande dame" of what became known as the philisophy of Libertarianism, or Individualism.

Rose was thrilled by the book's accomplishment. But she saw it as merely a start. Day after day, she studied and wrote and corresponded—following up every last lead to introduce others to her way of thinking. Her huge correspondence, which shared ideas, sharpened and honed her own understandings, was monumental. Meanwhile, as World War II heightened, so did what Rose termed "regimentation" of human lives.

How she hated red-tape, government snooping, and boring things like ration books! Asking, as she said, "some pert, snippy official" for permission to live was more than Rose would tolerate. And so on her three acres she raised great quantities of food to preserve (and even give away), to avoid a ration-book. She cut her expenses to the bone; the only writing she did was the editing of the National Economic Council's **Review of Books** for $60 per month—that let her escape from income tax. And she positively refused to be social secured—that, she thought, had led to Germany's downfall. "Did I ever tell you," she wrote Jasper Crane, "about the one, enraged, determined to get me into 'social security' who shouted at me, 'I am a PUBLIC SERVANT, I have no time to listen to YOU; you will do as I say or ELSE!? They are really very funny sometimes . . ."

In 1943, something occurred which Rose found less than funny. On a post card she responded unfavorably to an informal radio poll asking listeners' opinion of social security. Somehow, the card was intercepted in the mails —it never did reach New York City—and because Rose had likened social security to "national socialism" (Naziism), the FBI dispatched investigators to her quiet Danbury home. Rose was appalled and indignant when a zestful young trooper dared to question her Americanism. When she demanded to know just what the State Police had to do with "any opinion an American wants to express," the trooper informed her that what she thought and said added up to "subversive activity." Later on, recounting the event in a pamphlet she wrote for the National Economic Council, Rose recounted her reaction:

> A furious American rose to her full height. "You do not like my attitude? I am an American citizen. I hire you. And you have the insolence to question my attitude? What is this—the Gestapo?" I'm against all this so-

called social security—then I'm subversive as hell.

The incident was reported over the radio and over all the presswires. Rose succeeded in creating a national beehive, quite innocently, and publicly she warned all Americans to be vigilant of their rights. She asked: "Is there censorship within the American borders? If so, who is the censor? Who is obstructing the delivery of American mail? Precisely what is happening?"

By 1944, Rose was so distressed with what she saw as "regimentation" by New Deal and wartime tactics that she took another drastic step. She announced that she was "taking to the storm cellar until the Roosevelt administration blows over." She gave up her New York apartment, she ceased all writing so that not a tax dollar of hers would contribute to New Deal policies. And as an example to her readers, she revealed how very well one could live off the produce of even a small acreage like hers.

"I stopped writing fiction because I don't want to contribute to the New Deal," Rose explained when the news broke and reporters came swarming to question why the celebrated Mrs. Lane was retiring. "Income tax was the last straw," she said. "I don't see why I should work to support the Writer's War Board, the OWI and all such New Deal piffle while men are dying and there's work to be done at home." "They've tried price fixing since before the big flood and it's never worked," Rose went on. "The only effect is that it cuts down production and encourages black markets." When reporters queried just how Rose intended to survive, she led them down to her cellar. There, on the shelves 800 jars of canned produce glowed like gems. "That's genuine social security," Rose beamed. She also explained that she had bought an interest in a cow, a pig, and fortunately—her pioneer instincts served her well— she had a great quantity of flour stocked when rationing had set in.

Setting herself up as an example, Rose told readers that "the thing to do if you believe practices are wrong is to resist them. The American people did it with Prohibition.

The colonists did it when King George III tried to overtax them. The New Deal is going back to King George's economy and scarcity. We've got to resist. I feel very, very hard times are coming, but I also feel the people will pull through. I'm not pessimistic about that. The vote will have no effect until we have a politician who'll stand up and tell the truth."

Rose's battle against what she felt was the diminishment of American rights and principles was her passionate occupation for the last two decades of her life. She sought to educate and send forth "young Madisons and Jeffersons" all over the states and she truly felt that a great upsurge of Libertarianism would one day sweep America. Her idol Thomas Paine, had spoken of the indestructive "army of principles." Surely Rose did all she could in furthering true Americanism and if she felt proud of any of her many accomplishments, it was the contributions she had made in helping others make "the discovery of freedom."

VII.   BUSY YEARS, TOWARD THE END

In 1949, Rose's Father died far-off in Missouri. Almanzo Wilder was 92 and Laura was 82. Rose rushed to Mama Bess's side and together they realized that all they had was each other. Rose made an effort to spend as much time with her mother in Mansfield as possible; each winter she spent time at Rocky Ridge through the lonely cold months and when they were apart, Mama Bess and Rose exchanged an avalanche of letters.

The more Rose was home, the more she knew of her mother's huge fame and the influence of the "Little House" books. Rose saw the dozens of letters which came to her mother each day from unknown readers and summer day after summer day, cars from faraway would drive to meet Laura Ingalls Wilder. Although Mama Bess enjoyed her many honors—libraries were named for her, book awards were given her— perhaps Rose knew more than Laura ever could, what a wonderful gift the "Little House" book were to children everywhere.

Rose's own life in Danbury was a busy one. She was active in community life and projects; for instance her bread was for years a famous and regular contribution to the Danbury Fair. Visitors from near and far came to see and consult with Rose—most of them wanted to share in the wisdom of Rose's Libertarian thought. **Discovery of Freedom** continued to be enormously influential—a young professor in far-off Luxembourg had become so enthralled by Rose's ideas that he asked to translate the volume into European languages. And as always, Rose read widely, thought profoundly and corresponded extensively. It was her goal to eventually re-write and expand upon her original thesis in **Discovery.**

Along with intellectual pursuits, Rose loved her home-making. She still gardened and raised much of her own food and she was continually remodeling the Danbury house until it was a place of charm and modern comfort, yet never detracting from its antique simplicity. Re-doing the kitchen actually resulted in rearranging the whole house, it seemed. It had all started very innocently . . .

> Well, I had read Thoreau (Rose wrote) and I was living the simple life, but you know how it is. Every woman in every house is always dreaming of making it over. I often thought: If the pantry were gone, I wonder how big . . . That west wall all windows; afternoon sun flooding in. A big, sunny kitchen with a fireplace. Knotty pine, red-checked ging-ham. Oh well. But just to take down a wall and put in windows, that wouldn't be much, wouuld it? I said to my good friend an excellent carpenter: "Al, I've got an idea. Come look at the kitchen. Couldn't we . . . ?" Of course we could . . .

As the 1950's progressed, Rose's life formed a pleasant pattern: winters with Mama Bess in the Ozarks, summers and fall in Danbury. Mama Bess was nearing 90; it was hard to believe, but Rose herself was approaching 70. And then came the sad fall of 1956. Rose arrived home in time for Thanksgiving, and there at Rocky Ridge, she found Mama Bess very ill. Her heart was weak and diabetes was overtaking her. Sorrowfully, as the brown oak leaves blew and the cold rains fell, Rose and Laura seemed to realize that their time together was growing short. In the hospital in Springfield, Laura lay sick all through the holiday season, while Rose remained close by. Finally, they were together again, on Rocky Ridge. Through January of 1957, Laura seemed to gain a little, while Rose dashed around, keeping house, nursing, figuring out diabetic diet and trying to be cheerful. Soon, on February seventh, Mama Bess would be 90. That day came, but she fell asleep in the night and three days later, she was gone.

Alone, in the rambling, still house on Rocky Ridge, Rose prepared sadly to go home. Rocky Ridge no longer seemed like home to her, with both Mama Bess and Papa gone, so Rose was delighted when friends in Mansfield formed the Laura Ingalls Wilder Home Association, planning to preserve and open the Wilder home to all of Laura's many interested readers. Rose was most generous in making this project possible. When she knew it was in good hands, she left Mansfield for the last time, never to return.

Back home in Danbury, many months were to pass before Rose seemed herself again. But gradually, as life seeped back into her gardens and the Danbury countryside, enthusiasm returned to Rose. A "Freedom School" had been founded, out in Colorado—its aim was to offer seminars and information on Libertarian thought. Rose was delighted with the idea. She saw that books were acquired for the project and once even saved the school from foreclosure. And on two rare, wonderful occasions, Rose herself attended the Freedom School as a much-prized guest lecturer.

Around 1960, Rose resumed some professional writing. Eilene Tighe was back at **Woman's Day** and she prevailed upon Rose to once again do a series on American needlework. Rose thought it was a wonderful opportunity to really celebrate Americanism. Her monthly articles in 1961 and 1962, brought tens of thousands of letters into **Woman's Day;** Rose was proud when she told how they said "Thank you, THANK you, for American history, American spirit." Soon publishing houses were asking for the series in book form, but Rose was cautious. "Certainly some of them want to sabotage it," she noted. She knew very well that some Communist-entrenched publishers took manuscripts for the express purpose of printing, then repressing, American thought. Finally, Simon and Schuster won the book rights to Rose's **Book of American Needlework.** "Those boys are primarily money-makers," Rose wrote, so "I expect a good, continuing distribution, in addition to **Woman's Day's** already impressed 8,000,000 readers." Indeed, Simon and Schuster's production, in full color, in beautiful binding, matched Rose's beautiful prose that celebrated the rich American heritage of needlework.

Since her mother's death, Rose had been receiving the thousands of loving, appreciative letters from readers of the "Little House" books. Laura had patiently answered each letter and Rose tried to do the same. But to Rose came recurrent begging . . . "PLEASE, Mrs. Lane, tell us what happened next to Laura." And so Rose decided to partially answer that question in a book.

Among all of Laura's keepsakes exhibited in the museum now at Rocky Ridge was the little diary she had kept day-by day as the Wilders moved from Dakota to Mansfield in 1894. Rose felt that it would be just the sequel she could give to her mother's readers. As an added bonus, she wrote the setting for the diary; a before and after telling of life in DeSmet before the trip and life in Mansfield after they had arrived. Her loving memories, combined with Laura's own descriptions, were titled **On the Way Home,** a book which found its way to millions of readers in late 1962. But after that, Rose wrote no more about Mama Bess.

It was Rose's desire to progress on her revision and rewrite of **Discovery of Freedom** in the early 1960's—although she lived very much in the future, she knew that if she was to leave behind something substantial in the literature of liberty, she must not waste her time. Between visits and trips and letters and baking bread, Rose toiled away on **Discovery.** At her mammoth, personally designed desk upstairs in the study at Danbury, Rose poured out her ideas and opinions on the stacks of yellow typewriter paper. She even went off to Miami in the winter of 1962 to work uninterrupted on the book. At the Gold Dust Motel, no neighbors were dropping in, no phone calls were coming asking for "Laura's daughter's autograph," and no antics of her beloved little Maltese dogs were around to distract her from what she felt was her true mission. She made great strides in her retitled work, **The Discovery of Liberty.**

Looking at America carefully in the 1960's was somewhat disconcerting for someone with Rose's sensibilities. Communism, she felt, was a major threat. In Connecticut alone, Rose estimated that there were a thousand Communists. "Imagine, she mused, "if a thousand Communists came out to murder every influential person in Danbury." That, Rose warned, was what Communists called "the war of liberation," which had successfully been applied in many other countries. American economics appalled Rose: "We're in debt beyond all possibility of ever paying up; our money is being debauched and we're going to have a crash in comparison with which the one in the 1930's will seem like a Sunday School picnic." Despite her misgivings, Rose predicted that "This country will pull through. We're that kind of people."

As Communism and the Viet Nam war became ever increasing issues of discord and worry, Rose held out for aiding South Viet Nam. "If South Viet Nam goes, then all Southeast Asia will go," she predicted. "Then, Australia, the Philippines and Hawaii, where the Huks are already in waiting. The question is, do we want them on our soil?"

And then came a marvelous, dangerous exciting opportunity for Rose. The State Department had asked **Woman's Day** to send a correspondent over to Viet Nam to report the war from a "woman's view." And Eilene Tighe wanted Rose to take on the mission. Of course, she said yes. After all, Rose had traveled through Russia in box cars; she knew danger and she knew discomfort. The fact that she was 78 meant little to her. And so it was arranged. Rose Wilder Lane, veteran journalist would once again pack her dispatch case and go jaunting. As Rose rested in Washington prior to official briefing on a hot July day in 1965, the State department called off the trip. The last thing they wanted was a horror tale of a little old lady from America being mowed down on the streets of Saigon. But when Rose made it plain that she intended to fulfill her mission—whether she had to swim to Saigon—there was little anyone could do.

After "coping with Washington"—she had scant respect for bureaucracy, of course, Rose flew over the south seas to Viet Nam. As she always had in her reporting, even back in her Red Cross and Near East Relief days, Rose got close to the people; she learned their feelings and her perceptive mind read their fears and hopes. Through the hot, humid August days, Rose investigated. She flew on helecopter missions to observe what was happening on the ground and from the glass-roof of the Hotel Caravelle she watched the flashes of mortar fire. These adventurous times were reminiscent of those post-world War I days when she had rapidly skirted in and out of gun-range in Europe and Asia.

Rose's penetrating article, "August in Viet Nam" appeared in the December, 1965 issue of **Woman's Day** and in addition to the premiere reporting she did, her faith in freedom seemed to run through her words like a bright thread. Nearly a quarter century earlier, when democracy was opposing Naziism, Rose had closed her **Discovery of Freedom,** with this statement: "Win this war? Of course Americans will win this war. This is only war; there is more than that. Five generations have led the Revolution and the time is coming when Americans will set this world free." And, now, years later, Rose saw the struggle as being the same. "August in Viet Nam" concluded by saying that "Communism is **wrong.** So it is short term, it rises up swiftly as the quick flame, it is gone soon. As Hitler flared up and is gone. We stay; we survive. Because freedom is right and right is everlasting."

Back from Viet Nam, Rose was immersed in activity. First, she gave interviews, spoke at groups and wrote the Viet Nam article. Then she traveled cross-country with friends, out to the Grand Canyon. Then she moved. Not permanently; Danbury would always be home. But Rose bought a beautiful winter retreat" down in the Valley" of the Rio Grande, in Harlingen, Texas. On Woodland Drive, she settled down to remodel the ranch-style house and direct the landscaping of her park-like back-yard.

Harlingen was an escape from winter weather and Rose loved it. Her yard boasted orange and banana trees, along with fountains, rare blooming bushes and flowers and even a summer house with a revolving fan in the roof. Rose Lane was a much sought-after guest in Harlingen, as well as a wonderful hostess. She clearly enjoyed the lazy, warm days filled with friends, visitors and flowers. There she celebrated her eightieth birthday.

Rose had a new protege—lovely young Phan, the sister of her interpreter from Viet Nam, Rose urged Phan to come back to America with her for a college education, so on vacations and holidays Rose had company in Harlingen. "Bless these young people," Rose once said. She saw in them the dreams she and her breed of fellow **savantes** couldn't possibly live to carry out in helping set the world free.

Indeed, many of Rose's contemporaries were leaving the world. President Hoover, her long-time friend was gone; Dorothy Thompson , author, had died; often Rose read obituaries of editors, writers and artists she had once known. And while she always looked ahead, sometimes after her eightieth year had come, she lapsed into—not nostalgia—but a special kind of looking back. "In my ninth decade," she wrote,"it's a crown of something—not sorrow—to remember —not happier—days but days irrevocably gone."

Or . . .

When I was five years old, sitting one day in my grandmother's parlor in DeSmet on a footstool beside her rocking chair, and helping her sew carpet rags, after a long meditative silence I said dreamily, "I wish I had been there when Christ was crucified." My sincerely, deeply pious grandmother was (I now realize) deeply touched by this tender, young piety; I can recall the tone of her voice saying softly,

"Why, dear?" I replied, "So I could have cursed him and been the Wandering Jew."

I'm sure I recall the incident because of the inexplicable effect, upon my grandmother, of these candily innocent words. It was like an earthquake, a silent one. She **said** nothing. Somehow the air sort of crashed, terrifically.

But for most of my life it seemed ideal to be that mythical Wanderer. Imagine having been thirty-five years old—the perfect age; vigorously young yet somewhat recovering from being a total fool—since the year One, when Rome's Golden Age was beginning and Hellenic not yet wholly ended. Imagine being able to **remember** 1900 years, to be able to speak all languages, and to anticipate seeing all the rest of human history to the final destruction of this planet.

Only lately I've decided against that youthful ambition. Here I'm not yet ninety, and far from knowing all languages, I don't even know my own. Words I've relied upon all my life are quicksand under my feet. Just think of "square" for example. And hep, hip, hippie change so rapidly that they escape a grasp. And as for understanding people—Once I thought I had begun to, but now I give up . . .

Her marvelous zest for life was outliving her physical being, for when Rose was eighty-one, she, like Mama Bess, contracted diabetes. But she would not sit back and wait. She would travel around the world. She estimated that a good third of the globe remained unseen by her, and Rose was determined to remedy the situation. Even Spain—although she knew most of Europe well, that country had eluded her. And so, amidst invitations to weddings and showers from Harlingen friends during the spring of 1968, Rose started daily Spanish lessons.

Through the summer of 1968, while the bouganvillia, the hybiscus, and oleanders bloomed along with her favorite

Rose Wilder Lane in the bay window of her Connecticut home. Of this picture she wrote: "I dislike the exploitation of personalities so much that about forty years ago I began to refuse to have photographs taken or to allow photographers to take them. 'Woman's Day' did get one two years ago and used it in the magazine."

roses out in her garden, Rose Lane planned in the cool air-conditioned house. She set out an itinerary of three years. In the fall, she would leave for Europe and leisurely she would wend her way around the world until . . . Donald Giffen, the son of her good friends and neighbors, would accompany her on this last great adventure.

Fall came. Rose bid Harlingen good-by and headed north. She visited along the way. A special stop was made to see her lawyer-business manager and "honorary grandson," Roger MacBride in Virginia; then she visited the old, old friends from New York City days, the Floyd Dells. Finally, Rose was back in Danbury.

It was good to be back in the brick-floored kitchen and to sit with friends sipping coffee in the bay window. The fall colors were fading, but ahead lay new adventures. On October 30, Rose felt like making bread. Her bread was always famous around Danbury and she wanted to leave some for friends' freezers while she was away.

Evening came and Rose sat up late, chatting jovially with the friends who would take care of the Danbury house while she was gone. And then Rose said good-night and went to sleep. She did not awaken. Her long trip had been interrupted; replaced by another.

It is nearly impossible to sum up Rose's life in a few words, or sentences or paragraphs. She did so much which will last that her story can never really be over. Just as she said, "The longest lives are short; our work lasts longer."